To/

Take a trip back in time to the year you were born, 1942.

Happy 80th Birthday - enjoy reminiscing.

Lots of love,

80 YEARS AGO BACK IN 1942

World Population

2.3 BILLION

Britain population

48.2 MILLION

MAJOR WORLD LEADERS

UK- PM WINSTON CHURCHILL

US- PRESIDENT FRANKLIN D. ROOSEVELT

RUSSIA/SOVIET UNION - JOSEPH STALIN

ITALY - PM BENITO MUSSOLINI

GERMANY - ADOLF HITLER

CANADA -PM WILLIAM LYON MCKENZIE KING

SOUTH AFRICA - PM FIELD MARSHALL JAN CHRISTIAAN SMUTS

MEXICO - MANUEL AVILA CAMACHO

JAPAN - FUMIMARO KONOE / HIDEKI TOLO

2022

World Population

7.9 BILLION

Britain population

68 MILLION

You Have Been Loved for

YEARS

Thats 960 months

4174 Weeks | 29,220 days

701,280 hrs

42,076,800 MINUTES

2,524,608,000 SECONDS

and counting...

80 & Fabulous

BARBERA JOAN STRIESAND

BORN IN NEW YORK 24TH APRIL

SINGER, ACTRESS AND DIRECTOR

SIR PAUL McCARTNEY

BORN IN LIVERPOOL 28TH

SINGER/SONGWRITER

SIR WILLIAM "BILLY" CONNOLLY

BORN GLASGOW 24TH NOV 1942

COMEDIAN, MUSICIAN AND TV PRESENTER

BOB HOSKINS

BORN IN BURRY UK 26TH OCT 1942

ACTOR

HARRISON FORD

BORN IN CHICAGO 13TH JULY 1942

ACTOR

CAROLE KING

BORN NEW YORK 9TH FEB 1942

SINGER/SONGWRITER

Oscars

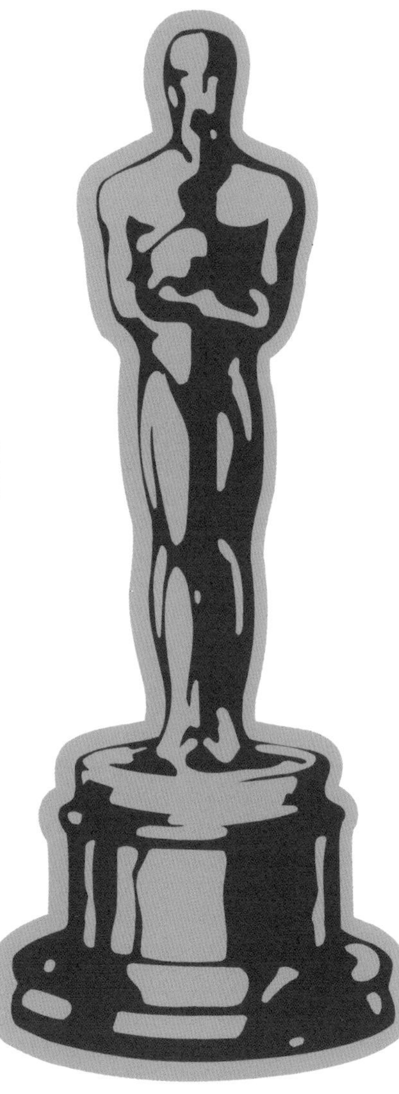

Best Actor

Gary Cooper

Sargeant York

Box Office

8.3 million USD

Best Original Screenplay

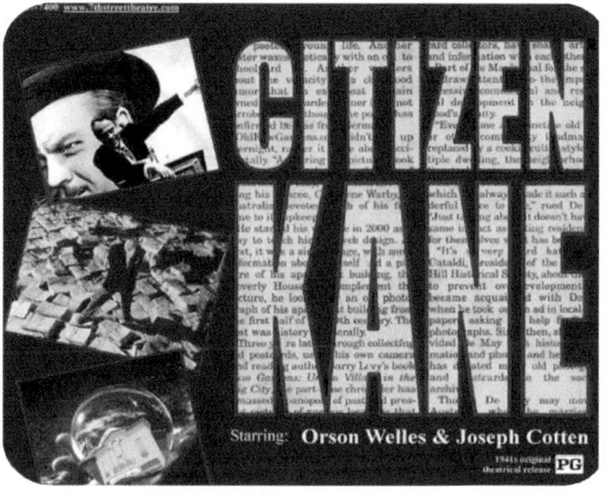

Best Actress

Joan Fortaine

Suspicion

Box Office

4.5 million USD

Average cost of living 1942

Average House £550 - In todays money thats £27,947

Average Salary £195 - In todays money thats £9,908

Average Car price £310 - In todays money thats £15,752

Average food shop £0.39 -In todays money thats £19.82

FOOD SHOPPING

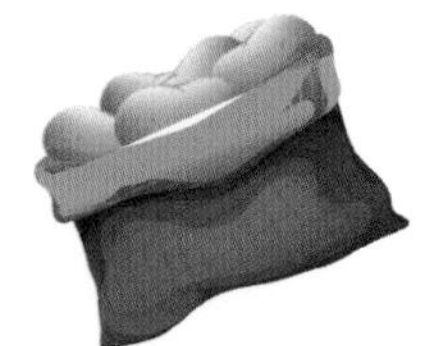

FLOUR 1.5KG £0.03 - £1.52 today

BREAD 1 LOAF £0.01 - 51p today

SUGAR 1KG £0.04 - £2.03 today

MILK 1PT £0.07 - £3.56 today

BUTTER 250G £0.04 - £2.03 today

CHEESE 400G £0.05 - £2.54 today

POTATOES 2.5KG £0.03 - £1.52 today

BACON 400G £0.12 - £6.10 today

- Total casualties for World War II are estimated between 70-80 million people, 80% of whom came from 4 countries – Russia, China, Germany & Poland. 50-55 million of the casualties were civilians, with the majority of those being women and children.
- Tokyo was the 3rd target for the atom bomb (if deemed necessary)
- Adolph Hitler's nephew, William Hitler served in the US Navy during World War II.
- To avoid using the German sounding name Hamburger during World War II, Americans used the name 'Liberty Steak'.
- In World War II British soldiers got a ration of 3 sheets of toilet paper per day. Americans got 22.
- Silly putty was accidentally discovered when a general Electric Engineer was trying to create synthetic rubber.

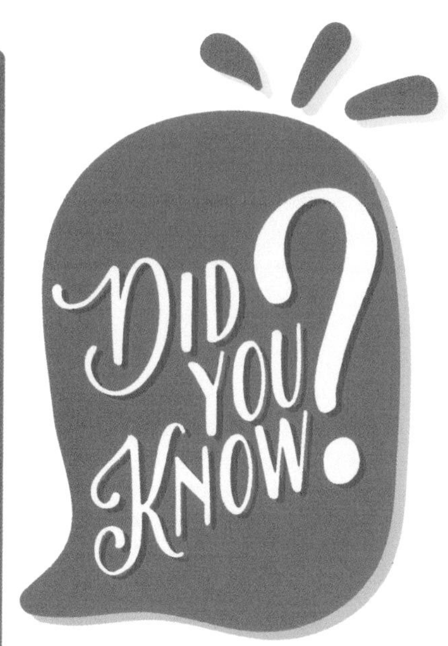

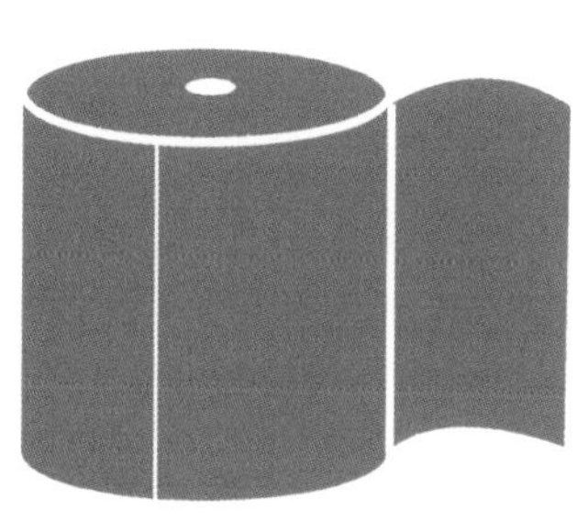

Welcome to the world -1942

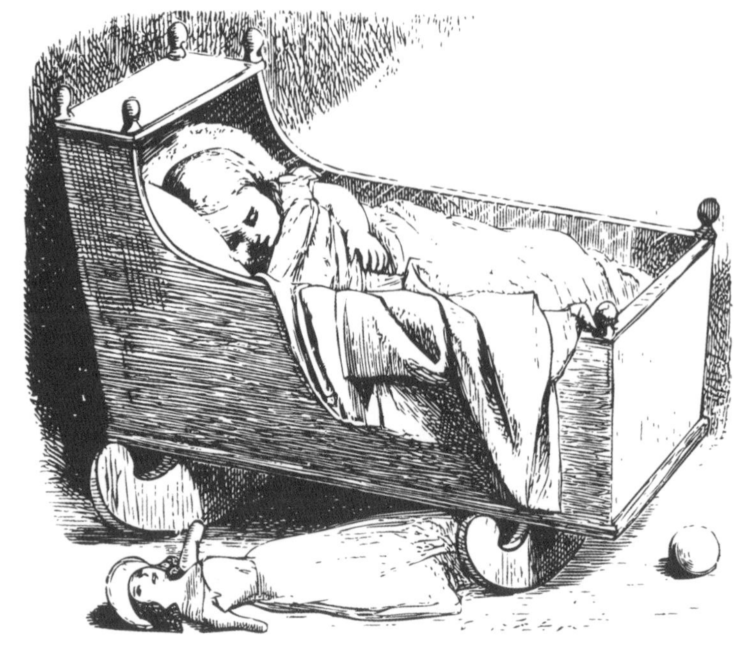

Girls
Mary
Barbara
Patricia
Carol
Linda
Judith
Betty
Nancy
Sandra
Carolyn

10 Most Popular Boys & Girls Names

War babies (1939-1945)

1942 recorded a low birth rate at approx. 770,000 births.

A normal year is approx 1 million births.

Boys
James
Robert
John
William
Richard
Charles
David
Thomas
Ronald
Donald

Books published 1942

The Stranger by Albert Camus

Mere Christianity by C.S.Lewis

The Body in the Library (Mrs Marple) by Agatha Christie

Mythology by Edith Hamilton

West with the Night by Beryl Markham

Children's Books 1940s

'The Shooting Star' Tin Tin book 10 by Herge

'The Little House' by Virginia Lee Burton

'The Runaway Bunny' by Margaret Wise Brown

'Five on a Treasure Island' Famous Five by Edith Blyton

Publishing in Wartime Britain

Books and the publishing industry are the lesser known victim of WWII. The devastating effects on the Country are well documented however there is less attention on the impact on the publishing industry. The industry was subjected to paper shortages, censorship restraints and a reduced workforce. Paper was rationed from 1940-1949. This proved a significant challenge in the continuation of a strong publishing industry. Despite this, the industry responded with a resolute determination to keep going and consequently through the war years there are some books we still regard as classics today. Understandably, throughout the war the demand for entertainment and distraction was high. This was in direct contrast to the ability to supply. Magazines were shorter in length, the margins and typeface fo books was poorer quality and overall the industry could not keep up with demand. This did however have a positive impact on the use of local libraries which found patronage at an all time high.

Films

No. 1256_778

THE TALK OF THE TOWN

When Nora says to the professor "he is as whiskered as the Smith Brothers", she is referring to a brand of cough drops manufactured by the Smith Brothers. The bottles had illustrations of the brothers on each bottle, both sporting full beards. This brand was the most popular brand for cough drops for over a Century.

No. 1256_779

BAMBI

Walt Disney produced many animated movie, Bambi was his personal favourite. Well known for disrupting the tradition, Walt insisted on children providing the voices for the characters instead of the usual adults mimicking children.

CASABLANCA

Due to Wartime restrictions during the filming of Casablanca, the crew were not able to film at the airport at night. They had to improvise with a soundstage and cut out aeroplanes to provide a perspective for the overall staging.

No. 1256_780

Films 1942

Cinemas during the War

When the war was first announced in 1939 cinemas were immediately closed. Within weeks the government realised people needed entertainment and they were reopened. Cinemas enjoyed a huge boom in attendance from 1942 onwards.

In 1942 cinema admissions rose to just over 1 billion and continued to rise through the war peaking at 1.5 billion in 1943, 1944 & 1945. Cinema going was the one of the nations favourite leisure activity and it proved to be an effective way of instructing and informing the nation during war years.

- Casablanca starring Humphrey Bogart, Ingrid Bergman & Claude Rains
- The Talk of The Town starring Cary Grant, Jea Arthur & Edgar Buchanan
- Mrs. Miniver starring Greer Garson, Walter Pidgeon & Richard Ney
- Road to Morocco starring Bob Hope, Dorothy Lamour & Anthony Quinn
- Woman of The Year starring Spencer Tracy, Katharine Hepburn & William Bendix
- Now, Voyager starring Bette Davis, Paul Henreid & Claude Rains
- Holiday Inn starring Bing Crosby, Fred Astaire & Marjorie Reynolds
- Saboteur Sterling Norman Lloyd, Priscilla Lane & Robert Cummings
- Across the Pacific starring Mary Astor, Humphrey Bogart & Sydney Greenstreet
- For Me and my Gal starring Judy Garland, Gene Kelly & George Murphy

Music

Harry Lillis "Bing" Crosby Jr.

American Singer, Comedian and Actor. The first multimedia star.

Born 3rd May 1903 in Washington USA.

Biggest hit was the recording of Irving Berlin's White Christmas, first broadcast on Christmas day 1941, it sold over 50 million copies, Topping the charts in three different years, 1942, 45 and 47

Alton Glenn Miller was an American Big Band Trombonist, Composer and Band Leader in the 40s Swing era. Th Best selling Artist from 1939-1942, Miller scored 16 number ones and 69 top 10 hits, beating Elvis who had 38 top 10s and the Beatles who had 33 t 10s.

No 1's

The official UK pop charts based on record sales didn't begin until November 1952. Statistics for records before this date are taken from weekly pop chart based on the sales of the sheet music, which was published by melody maker and broadcast by radio Luxembourg.

3rd Jan-1 Jan	Bless You	Ink Spots
3rd Jan-6th Feb	Chattannooga Choo Choo	Glenn Miller
7th Feb-13th Feb	A String of Pearls	Glenn Miller
14th Feb-20th Feb	Blues in the Night	Woody Herman
21st Feb-27th Feb	A String of Pearls	Glenn Miller
28th Feb-8th May	Moonlight Cocktail	Glenn Miller
9th May-19t	Tangerine	Jimmy Dorsey
20th Jun-17th Jul	Sleepy lagoon	Harry James
18th Jul-11th Sep	Jingle Jangle Jingle	Kay Kyser
12th Sep-30th Oct	Ive got a Gal in	Glenn Miller
31st Oct-1st Jan	White Christmas	Bing Crosby

Fashion

The first half of the '40s fashion was heavily impacted by the War. The combination of women & men regularly wearing uniform and the effect of rationing defined fashion for the first 5 years. The '20s defined by flapper girls and Art Deco, the '30s by comparison saw a softer silhouette, a more conservative approach with some Hollywood Glamour inspiration from films.

Not surprisingly the silhouette of the early '40s had a no nonsense feel, military style influenced daywear. Playsuits and skirt suits were particularly popular. There was a lack of embellishment (due to rationing) . Despite this apparent lack of innovation, the '40s military style is still admired today. The close fitting waist dresses and utilitarian embellishments were created in a way that flattered the figure looked feminine while practical at the same time.

Fashion

Ration coupon allocation:

By 1941, it became compulsary for all utility clothes to be marked 'CC41'. Each person was allocated 66 coupons to last one year.

- Ladies dress 11 coupons
- Pair of stockings 2 coupons
- Mans shirt 8 coupons
- Footwear - typically 7 coupons

Additional coupons were provided for children, with the obvious reason that they grew out of clothes more quickly. Although you may remember having to wear clothes a bit too big with your Mum saying "you'll grow into them!"

1940s mens clothing restrictions meant that jackets could not have pleated backs, metal zippers or buttons, feature raglan sleeves, or have half belts. Most men kept their clothing from the 1930s and wore them through the early '40s. It was a sign of support for the war to be seen in your pre-war suits.

Famous for
fine-Quality
"Nell Gwyn"
Marmalade
AND FRESH FRUIT JAMS BY Crosbie's

TAKES THE
STRAIN
The war years are reflected in the nervous conditions of people everywhere. 'SANATOGEN' Tonic Wine is a restorative, combining the qualities of a rich full-bodied wine with the active tonic properties of 'SANATOGEN' Nerve Tonic Food.
'SANATOGEN'
TONIC WINE
The word "SANATOGEN" is a Registered Trade Mark
per 10/- bottle

"Mars
ARE
MARVELLOUS"
You'll certainly agree! Just taste these chunks of sheer delicious goodness made with chocolate to sustain, glucose to energise, milk to nourish you.
4½d.

USE A LITTLE
Gumption
SMOOTH PASTE
CLEANSER
CLEANS BATHS,
PAINT, FLOORS Etc.
CONTAINS GLYCERINE
TO KEEP YOUR HANDS SOFT
1/-
AND
2/6

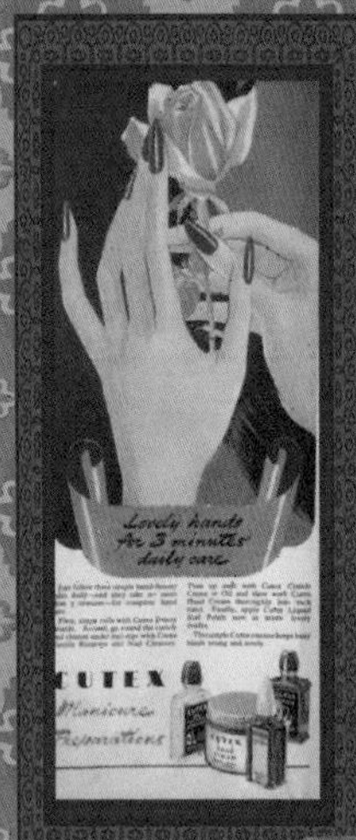
Lovely hands
for 3 minutes
daily care
CUTEX

Me for
McDougall's
SELF-RAISING
flour
- still the surest!

ONE-O-ONE
Cleans Kitchen Utensils easily
From Grocers and Oilmen
Use more sparingly than ever, supplies are further restricted

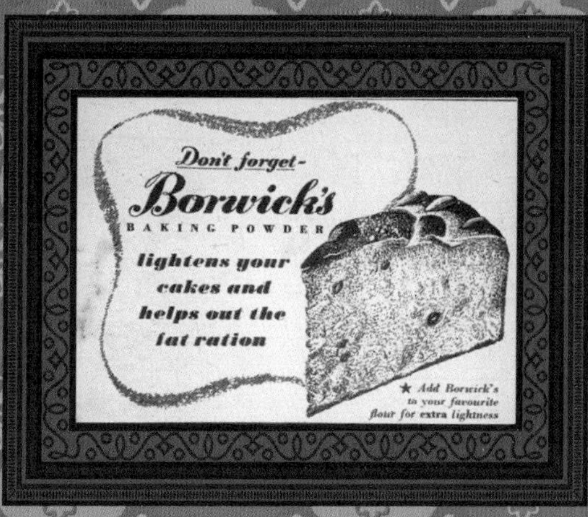
Don't forget-
Borwick's
BAKING POWDER
lightens your cakes and helps out the fat ration
★ Add Borwick's to your favourite flour for extra lightness

Sweet as Sugar!
NATURAL Nº1 Processed PEAS
WILLER & RILEY (1910) LTD
BOSTON · LINCS.

"How my feet do hate queues!"
Then why not walk into the nearest Scholl Depot and let us make your feet queueproof! Corns, callouses, bunions—all common foot ailments—can quickly be eased. Weak arches can be re-balanced with light flexible arch supports, which stop the aching and allow you to walk and stand in comfort. All over the world, people with every kind of foot trouble know the efficiency of Scholl methods. Come in and let us examine your feet. We have branches everywhere. Scholl Foot Aids are sold by all chemists, shoe-dealers, stores and all Scholl Depots.
SCHOLL FOOT COMFORT SERVICE
254 REGENT STREET, LONDON W1
Branches everywhere
it spreads like butter!
...and it actually contains butter
Dairylea Fried Sandwiches
KRAFT
DAIRYLEA CHEESE SPREAD

IS THAT A PERSIL-WHITE BUNNY?
I'M GOING TO PAINT HIM PERSIL-BRIGHT
PERSIL-WHITE
PERSIL-BRIGHT

LOOK!
Butywave shampoo brings out the hidden beauty of the hair. Produces brilliant high lights, natural waviness and a soft lustre of health.
BUTYWAVE
SHAMPOO—Just suits my hair!

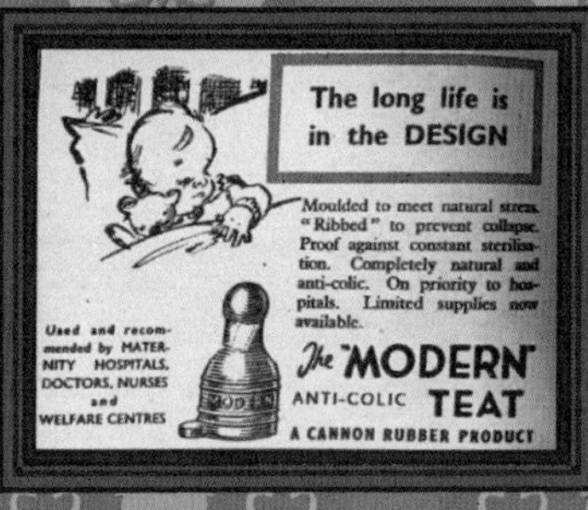
The long life is in the DESIGN
Moulded to meet natural stress. "Ribbed" to prevent collapse. Proof against constant sterilisation. Completely natural and anti-colic. On priority to hospitals. Limited supplies now available.
Used and recommended by MATERNITY HOSPITALS, DOCTORS, NURSES and WELFARE CENTRES
The "MODERN" ANTI-COLIC TEAT
A CANNON RUBBER PRODUCT

Stephenson's
FURNITURE CREAM & FLOOR POLISH
brings the sun into your home
STEPHENSON'S
NonSmear FLOOR POLISH

Sports during the War

During 1942, there was no major football competitions in England, Scotland or France due to World War II. Regional leagues were played throughout England and Scotland.

Sport played a vital role throughout the War time years for civilians and for the armed forces. Football in particular in the U.K provided a much welcome distraction, and although the main competitions were cancelled there was no lack of games both amateur and professional throughout the early '40s.

British Army & Sports

Throughout history, British armies have long utilised sports for a variety of reasons. The most obvious is to develop the fitness of their soldiers. However, there are also other factors which enhance teamwork and mental well-being.

International sports news

- Golf Masters - Bryon Nelson
- Hale American National Open - Ben Hogan
- Gold US PGA - Sam Snead
- Tennis US national - Fred Schroeder & Pauline Betz
- Baseball World Series - St Louis Cardinals

Competitions have been reported between soldiers on the front line and in POW camps. Sports provided a welcome temporary respite from a time of great stress.

Over 2 million soldiers were wounded in the First World War. Advances in medical intervention (artificial limbs, facial reconstruction and therapy) offered a degree of rehabilitation, but many men were left to fend for themselves and suffered great hardships, unable to provide for their families and suffering from PTSD with little support.

When WWII ended the rehabilitation programme had improved considerably. There was a concerted effort to encourage soldiers to participate in sports as an essential part fo their recovery programme.

The 1948 Olympic games, were held in London. Dr Ludwig Guttman took it upon himself to organise a competition for soldiers who had spinal injuries. The 'International Wheelchair Games' was the beginning of what is now the Paralympic games. The mascot for the London 2012 Paralympics was called 'Mandeville' in honour of Dr Guttman. The mascot tradition continues to this day.

War Time Rations

Food rationing was in place throughout 1942. On January 8th 1940 it began with bacon, ham, sugar and butter. Later in 1940 meat, tea, margarine, cooking fats and cheese were rationed. In 1941 jam, marmalade, treacle and syrup were added to the list. Then in June 1941 the distribution of eggs was controlled. In August 1941 manual workers were given an extra cheese allowance. In December 1941 national dried milk and a vitamin welfare scheme was introduced. By mid 1942 everything with the exception of vegetables, fruit, fish and bread.

Despite the war ending in 1945 (when you were just 3) food rationing was still in place until 4th July 1954 which totals 14 years of food rations. As a child you'll likely remember the joy when sweet rationing finally ended in 1953 (an attempt had been made to end sweet rationing in 1949 but lasted for only months as feverish demand far outweighed supply!).

WW2 Rations 1942: per one person (adult)
Butter: 50g (2oz)
Bacon or ham: 100g (4oz)
Margarine: 100g (4oz)
Cooking fat/lard: 100g (4oz)
Sugar: 225g (8oz).
Meat: To the value of 1/2d and sometimes 1/10d – about 1lb (450g) to 12ozs (350g)
Milk: 3 pints (1800ml) occasionally dropping to 2 pints (1200ml).
Cheese: 2oz (50g) rising to 8oz (225g)
Eggs: 1 fresh egg a week.
Tea: 50g (2oz).
Jam: 450g (1lb) every two months.
Dried eggs: 1 packet (12 eggs) every four weeks.
Sweets & Chocolate: 350g (12oz) every four weeks

Ration Recipe

Wartime Spiced Biscuits

- 225g self raising flour
- 1/4 teaspoon mixed spice
- 1 pinch salt
- 2 tablespoons caster sugar
- 1 dessertspoon dried egg
- 280g margarine
- 2 tablespoons chopped sultanas
- 2 tablespoons raisins
- 1 dessertspoon milk, or more if needed

1. Preheat the oven to 190 C
2. Mix the dried ingredients. Rub the margarine into the mixture until it looks fine breadcrumbs. Add the fruit and then the milk to form a dough. Turn the dough out and roll out to 1cm thickness. Cut into rounds.
3. Bake in the oven for 10 to 15 minutes until golden brown.

These would have been made as a treat. The margarine is almost 3 adults full allowance for a week. Do you remember being treated to some spiced biscuits? Try some at home and bring back the memories.

Toys

The 1940s began with Britain in the midst of the Second World War . The war period was one of great austerity, with shortages of all consumer goods and materials. The toy industry was subject to the same restrictions as other industries and rationing continued long after the war ended. Most children played with toys which had been handed down from older children or made at home.

Where possible, some firms, such as Nicol Toys, were able to continue production throughout the war. Plimpton Engineering, the manufacturers of the construction set Bayko, used clever substitutes for materials in the toy kits. The aesthetic suffered however this wasn't really a major concern for them or the customers. By the end of 1941 toy production had to stop and efforts were focused entirely to the war effort, producing goods including parts for Wellington bombers.

Children throughout all the major cities in Britain had to endure nightly bombing. The impact was becoming severe, especially without games and toys to entertain and distract them. Sir William Stephenson, chairman of Woolworths and head of Aircraft Production was requested to find a source for materials to increase toy production. He decided to approach Lod Beaverbrook with a proposition that could solve the issue.

Toys

Lord Beaverbrook (who was then the publisher of the Daily Express) was approached by his staff to help source paper pulp that could be used to replace traditional materials for toy production. He agreed on the requirement that Woolworths would keep their cost to just sixpence (2½p) for the duration of the war. Stephenson accepted those terms, and Woolworths were able to produce and sell sets that included: a cardboard boxing game which pitted the PM Winston Churchill against the villain Adolf Hitler, Lumar patriotic jigsaw puzzles and also popular card games. These clever alternatives toys became increasingly important as the war progressed because, from 1942, the toy industry was not allowed to use metal in any toy production.

Did you Know?

The British Secret Intelligence had John Waddington Ltd, create a very unique version of the popular board game. Like something from a great spy film they hid real maps, compasses, real German money and other objects the POW would find useful in their endeavours to escape! These were distributed by fake charity groups.

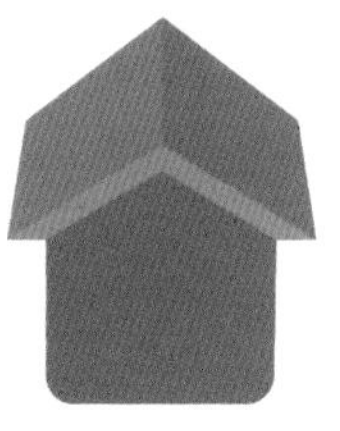

World Events 1942

JAN

Operation Typhoon

On January 7th Germany failed to take Moscow

Actress Carole Lombard is killed

American film actress is killed on TWA flight alongside her mother and 16 others. She was on tour promoting War Bonds. Recently Carole was nominated the 16th Greatest Actress of all time.

Declaration of the UN

In January, 26 nations sign the declaration of the UN. The treaty was signed in Washington, D.C. It held each nation to adhering to the Atlantic charter.

Henry Ford

Ford is granted a patent for a plastic car. The benefits being it is 30% lighter than a regular car.

Pilot Helmet Schenk

Heinkel test pilot, Helmut Schenk is successful in his mission to escape from an aircraft using an ejection seat.

War Relocation Authority

Franklin D.Roosevelt, President of U.S implements the Executive Order creating the WRA that relocates 120,000 Japanese and people with Japanese ancestry living in America, many for the duration of the war.

Singapore falls to Japan

Singapore falls to Japan in February, with approximately 25,00 prisoners taken.

MAR

WWII - Nazi, the Reichstag

The last meeting of the Reichstag dissolves itself giving absolute power to Adolf Hitler. Hitler is given the authority and control of the life and death of every German citizen.

Academy Awards

14th Academy awards are held in Los Angeles. The Best Picture goes to 'How Green Was My Valley'.

World events

Princess Elizabeth

The young Princess signs up for War Service.

Anne Frank

The first entry in Anne Franks diary is recorded as June 12th.

JUN

Nuclear Reactor

He first Nuclear accident in history is recorded on the 23rd June. The nuclear reactor L-IV explodes causing a reactor fire

Anne Frank

Records show Anne Franks family went into hiding on the 6th July. They hid in the attic above her fathers office in a warehouse in Amsterdam.

AUG

Radio controlled Torpedos

Hedy Lamarr and George Antheil register a patent for a radio controlled torpedo. The patent is granted however is not in use until 1962 during the Cuban Missile Crisis.

Plutonium

On August 20th at the Metallurgical Laboratory, Plutonium is isolated for the first time.

Battle of Midway

American naval success, marks an important turning point in the Pacific War.

Bambi

April 12th - Bambi is released.

World Events 1942

Zofia Kossak-Szczucka

Polish writer and head of the underground organisation Front for the Rebirth of Poland, published a book to protest about the mass murder of the Jewish population in German-occupied Poland.

Operation Pluto

The river Medwey is used to test the plan to construct oil pipelines under the English Channel.

OXFAM founded

The Oxford Committee for Famine Relief is founded on the 31st July.

Luxembourgish general strike

Protests about forced conscription take place in luxembourg. It was a display of passive resistance and was met with force by German authorities. 21 strikers were sentenced to death.

WAVES

WAVES (Women accepted for volunteer emergency service)as part of the US naval reserve, is signed into law.

US Scrap days

Beginning October 1942, the U.S government began a Scrap days campaign. Encouraging people to donate scrap items that could be repurposed and used in the War effort.

WAFS

The Women's Auxiliary Ferrying Squadron (WAFS) is established in the U.S.

World events

A-4 Rocket launch

The first man made object to reach space is the A-4 Rocket. Launched in Germany, it flew 147 kilometres with an altitude of 84.5 Km.

The Holocaust - Oct

Political figureheads in the U.K hold a public meeting to display their anger over the persecution of the Jewish people at the hand of the Nazi regime.

Enigma retrieval

Brave British soldiers board a sinking U boat (U-559) while it sinks to retrieve it's Enigma machine along with the codebooks.

Casablanca

Premiere of the now classic film, takes place in the Hollywood Theatre in New York City.

Times Square

For the first time since it began it's much loved tradition, the Times Square Ball was not dropped at midnight. Instead, there was a one minute silence, followed by a recording of bells ringing.

Alaskan Highway

Also known as the Alcan Highway, the Alaskan highway, connecting Alaska to Canada, was finally completed, however it was not in use until a year later 1943.

Manhattan Project

At the University of Chicago, a team of scientists initiate the first self-sustaining nuclear chain

Inventions from the early 40s

The 1940s can reasonably be referred to as one of most important decades of the past century. Undeniably the War impacted in a way that would impact generations to come however it was also the technology that was created as a direct result of the war that would go on to change our lives forever. The events in the 1940s are still remembered today and the inventions that resulted have impacted society to the present day.

Aerosol can

The concept of an aerosol goes back to the 1790s, the first patent granted in 1927 however it wasn't until 1941 that the aerosol can was first put to efficient use by Lyle Goodhue & William Sullivan who are widely credited as inventors of the modern spray can. It was created during WWII as a means to kill malaria carrying bugs for soldiers.

Biomimicry

Velcro

A fascinating story of inspiration. Inventor George de Mentral was out walking his dogs and noticed how effectively the burrs attached to his dog. A flash of inspiration resulted in his developing velcro-an amazing multi-purpose material.

CBS & Peter Goldmark pioneered a system which transmitted an image in each of the 3 primary colours. Their TV was based on John Logie Bairds designs.

Mobile Phones

Surprised? While the first commercially viable phone didn't come into existence until 1983 it was way back in 1947 that T&T proposed the allocation of radio-spectrum frequencies with the intention of widespread telephone service. Bell Laboratories that introduced the idea of cellular comms in 1947 with police car technology.

The Jeep

Was designed in 1940 in just 18 hrs by Karl Probst. Production of the first prototype took just 72 days.

The Z3 - May 12th 1941

Konrad Zuse The Z3 was the world's first working programmable, fully automatic digital computer. It was also the first computer-controlled by software. The computer itself was built with 2,600 relays implementing a 22-bit word length that operated at A clock frequency of approximately 4-5 Hz.

Inventions from the early 40s

Atomic Bomb

"I am become Death, the destroyer of worlds." The words that theoretical physicist, J. Robert Oppenheimer, reportedly said after he saw the result of his invention. The quote comes from a Hindu famous scripture, also said to be a mistranslation. Without a doubt, the atomic bomb and its destructive power were life changing, impacting the course of WWII, the coming Cold War and the course of our history.

The Kidney Dialysis Machine

Willem Johan Pim Kolff was a pioneer in the field of hemodialysis and field of artificial organs. During WWII he made major discoveries in the field of kidney dialysis; the result of which would go on to save countless lives.

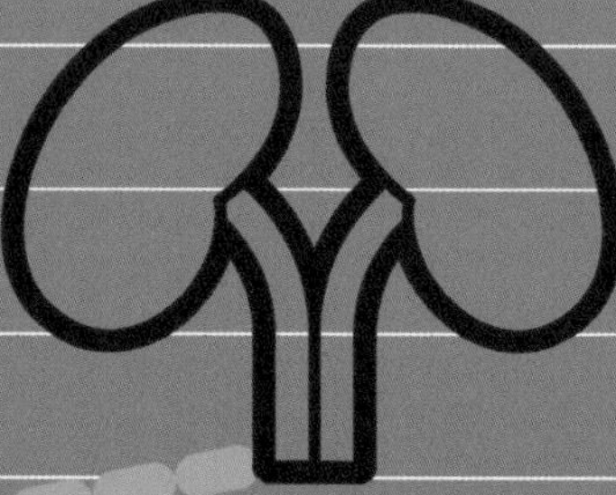

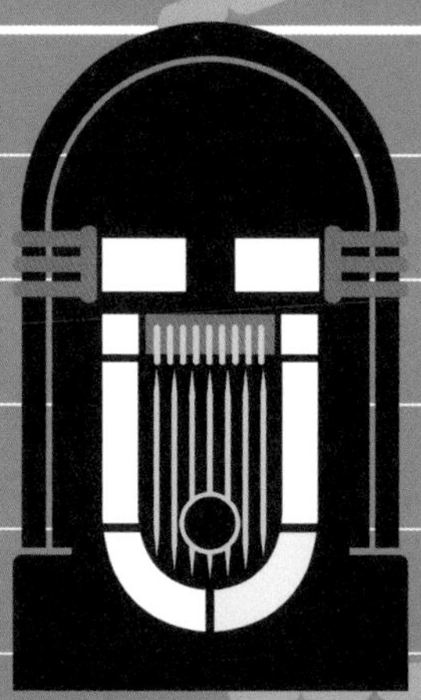

The Juke Box

The first jukebox was in play in 1890s, however the jukebox as you will think of it didn't appear until the 1940s. During the 40's it's estimated that two thirds of all records in USA were played on jukeboxes, such was their popularity.

Microwave

Percy Spence is the man that brought the microwave over into existence in 1947. The invention was actually based off of radar technology that was created during the war. However, it was still far from the microwave that you know today. The countertop friendly microwave did not make its way to the market until 1967.

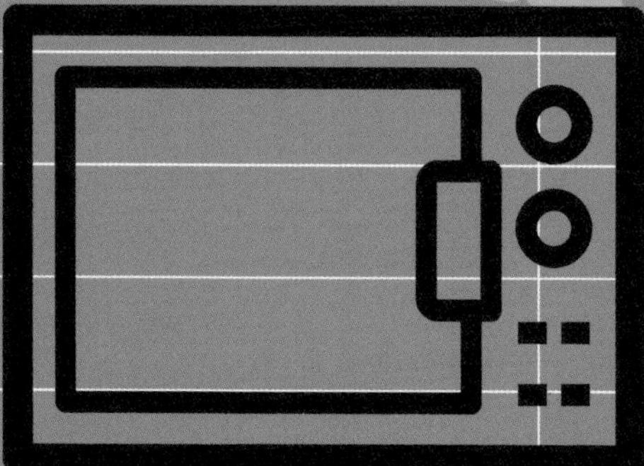

The V campaign

The famous symbol that boosted morale of the British people during the darkest days of World War Two. Prime Minister Winston Churchill made the V for Victory hand gesture one of the most recognisable images of the war.

Today, the gesture is more commonly known as 'peace' however back in 1941 it held much more power.

The famous wartime symbol is now synonymous with Churchill, although surprisingly he wasn't the one who came up with it.

The powerful sign was first used in Belgium a year before it moved across Europe and then to Britain. Winston Churchill first used the V forVictory sign on July 19, 1941.

Churchill often got confused and showed the hand symbol with the palm facing inwards. In true Churchill style, even when he was told of the profanity of using the hand gesture, he continued to use it anyway.

Loose Lips Sink Ships

Propaganda & advertising during the War.

The government reused many of the WWI campaigns. The most effective were the posters designed to persuade the British public to get on board with various different requests. From pro war projects to fostering hostility towards Hitler, promoting evacuation or volunteer roles and raising support for the allies, the messages were all part of the propaganda employed to help win the war. The use of print, radio and cinema advertising ensured that the message that Hitler was just at the doorstep and everyone must play their part, was communicated in various ways and was effective. Their was a clever mix of fear inducing messages alongside patriotic 'you can do your bit'.

Dig For Victory - Campaign by the Ministry of Food

In 1939 only 30% of the food consumed in Britain was homegrown. The country had already got used to cheap food imports. The grow your own and dig for victory campaigns were an essential part of ensuring the nation was fed. By 1941 there was over 1.4 million allotments producing a whopping tonne of vegetables per year.

Make Do and Mend

Clothes rationing began in June 1941. The advertising campaign that followed encouraged people to be resourceful.

The Make Do and Mend campaign was launched by the Board of Trade. It was influential in promoting people to adapt their existing wardrobe rather than look for new clothing.

Artists were brought in to make sure the posters were visually appealing and ensured the message was clear.

Evacuation

During 1941 many British children were living with host families as evacuees. By the end of the war around 3.5 million children had been evacuated.

There were 3 rounds of evacuation the first in 1939. However initially as there were no immediate bombings the children came home. During the blitz of autumn 1940 children were again sent away for safety.

Many pregnant women were also evacuated - there were many babies born in the countryside that Retuned to the city when it was deemed safe.

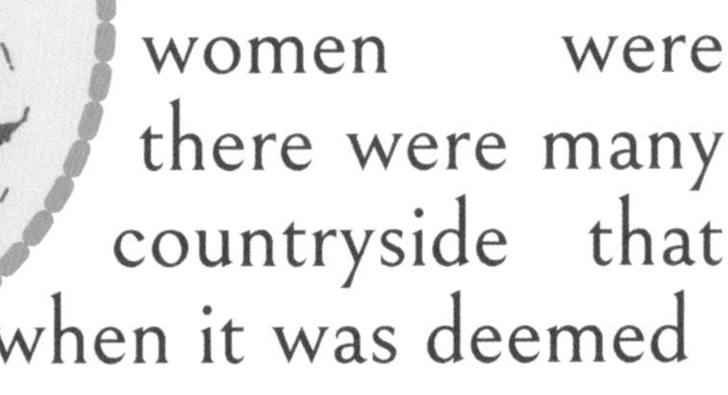

The Blitz

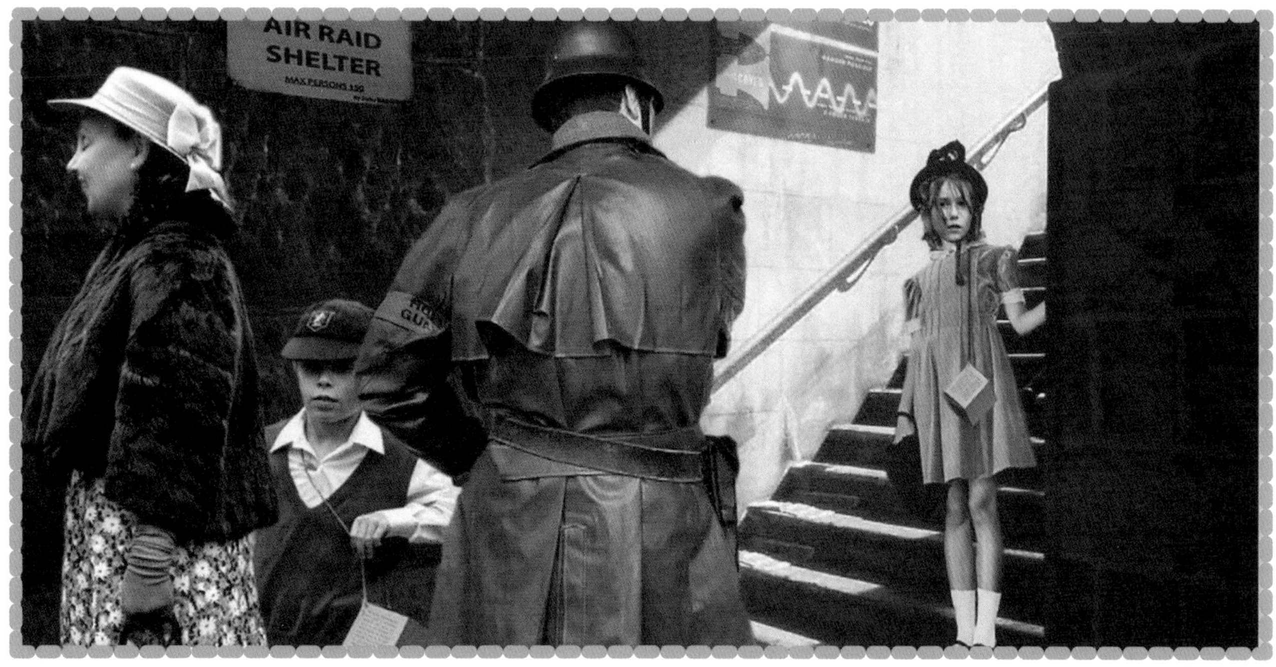

The incessant bombing attacks on London and other cities is referred to as the 'Blitz'. There was 9 months of constant bombings from late 1940 to Spring 1941. German bombers targeted cities, ports and industrial areas.

London was the prime target, and was hit every day and night for 11 weeks straight. It was devastating - one third of London was destroyed. Swansea, Cardiff, Bristol, Southampton, Plymouth, Birmingham, Coventry and Liverpool also suffered terrible attacks.

One raid on Coventry in November 1940 was by far the worst air raid on record; 4,330 homes destroyed and 554 people were tragically killed.

DIG FOR VICTORY

They use me on the kitchen front

THE
SURREY
HOUNDS
DUNLOP

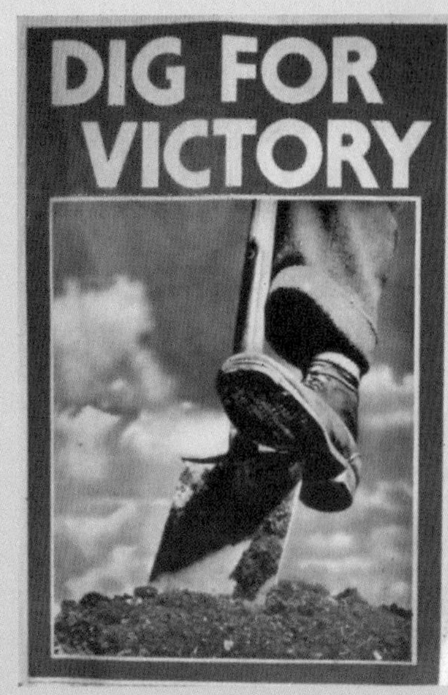

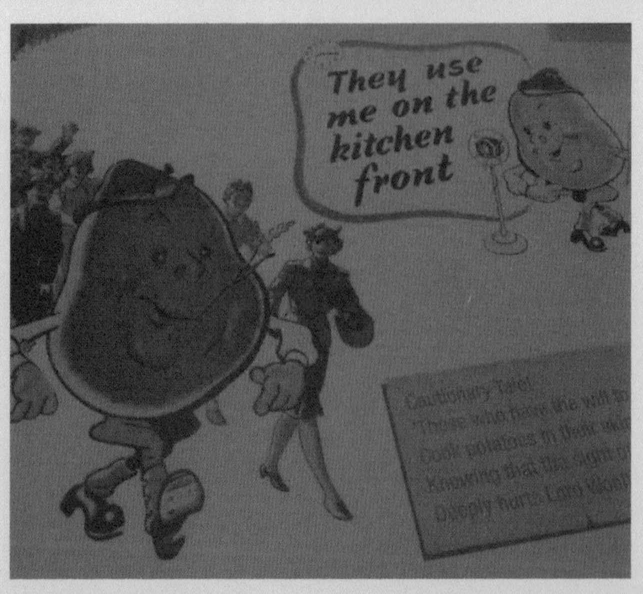

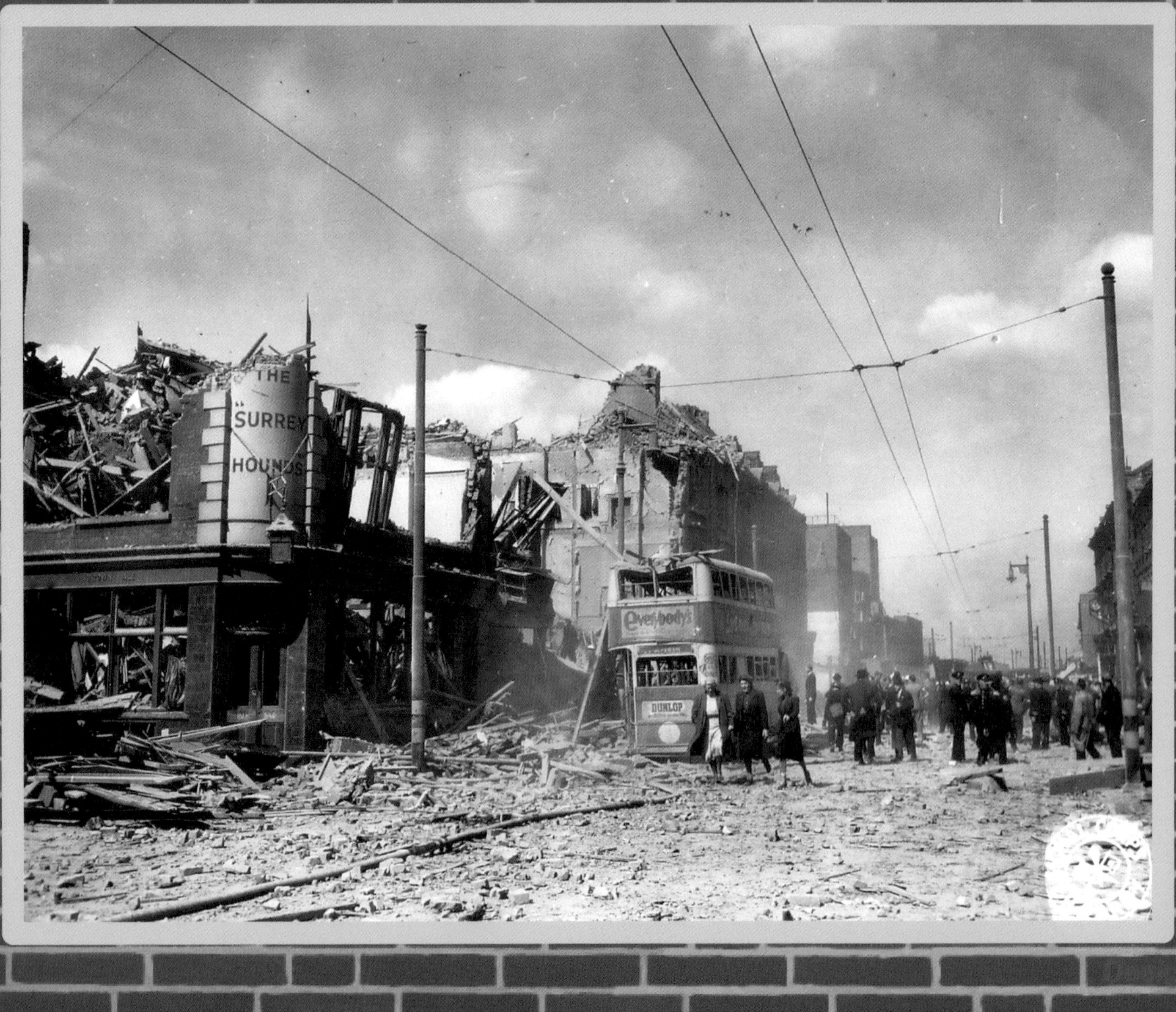

BY APPOINTMENT
CONCENTRATED BEEF
A MEAL IN A MOMENT
OXO
CUBE
OXO
CONCENTRATED BEEF
OXO
CUBE
A MEAL IN A MOMENT
IT'S 'MEAT & DRINK' TO YOU

Where our men are fighting
OUR FOOD IS FIGHTING
BUY WISELY – COOK CAREFULLY – STORE CAREFULLY – USE LEFTOVERS

...SABOTAGE
CAN OUTWEIGH
PRODUCTION
IF YOU QUESTION IT-REPORT IT!
COME CALL 242 or WRITE INTELLIGENCE OFFICER.

CITY OF LONDON POLICE

DANGER

UNEXPLODED BOMB

BETTER POT-LUCK
with Churchill today
THAN HUMBLE PIE
under Hitler tomorrow
DON'T WASTE FOOD!

PUBLIC SHELTERS
IN VAULTS
UNDER PAVEMENTS
IN THIS STREET

UNDERGROUND
THIS WAY
TO THE
AIR RAID SHELTER
WESTON STREET SE1
LONDON BOROUGH OF SOUTHWARK

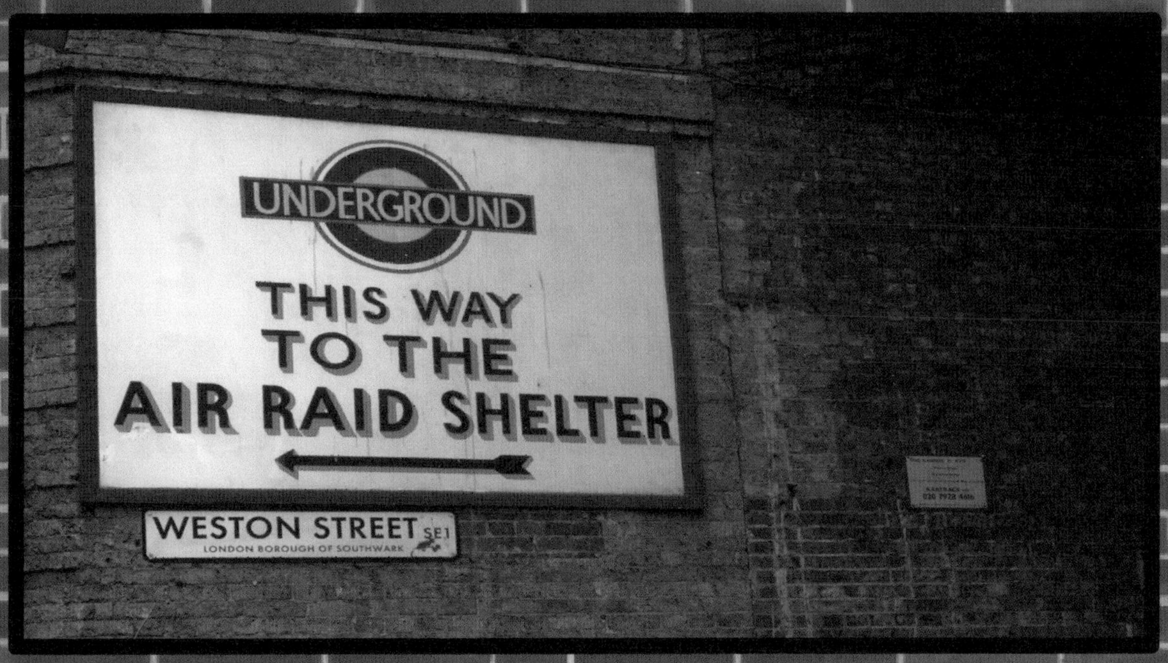

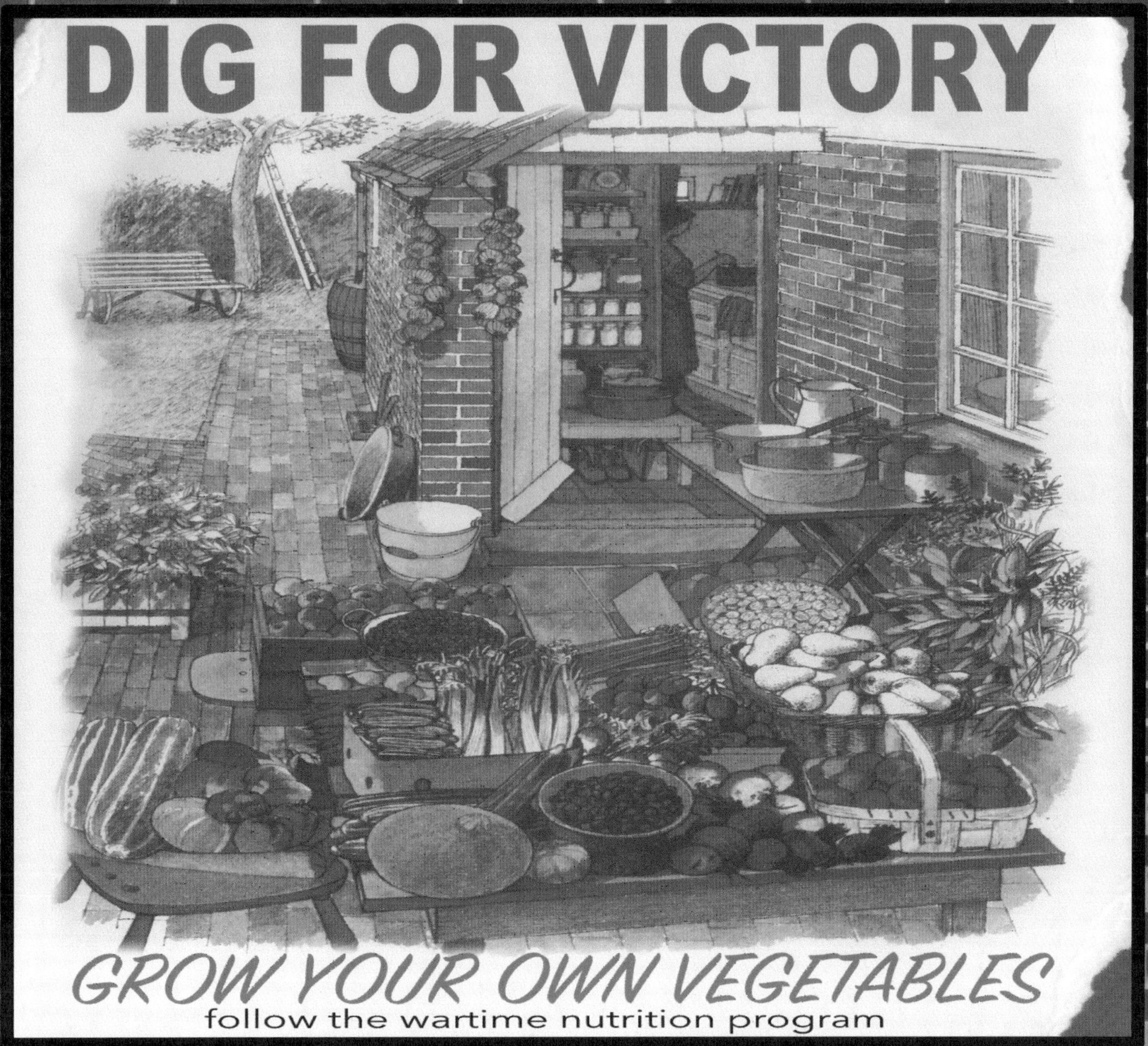

DIG FOR VICTORY
GROW YOUR OWN VEGETABLES
follow the wartime nutrition program

The legal stuff

Attribution for photo images goes to the following talented photographers under the creative commons licenses specified:

Attribution 4.0 International (CC BY 4.0)
Attribution-ShareAlike 4.0 International (CC BY-SA 4.0)

Various photo images are licensed under the following https://creativecommons.org/licenses/by/2.0

www.flickr.com/photos/bongonian/8720834120

www.flickr.com/photos/wainwell7XrQWU-bDU2sK-bqZ5PA-bE8L5K-cl6mgY-brdRCf-bE8N52-brdUrQ-cl6tWy-brdQrW-brdQaf

https://www.flickr.com/photos/67331818@N03/8435815214

https://www.flickr.com/photos/39415781@N06/5121548642

https://www.flickr.com/photo25797459@N06/3255446185

https://www.flickr.com/photos/28884294@N04/4397471133

https://www.flickr.com/photos/37996637875@N01/1129554100

https://commons.wikimedia.org/index.php?curid=50788264

https://www.flickr.com/photos/47201412@N02/6634268777

https://www.flickr.com/photos/41525293@N00/4488405042

https://www.flickr.com/photos/39735679@N00/443628643

ttps://www.flickr.com/photos/24592131@N00/32399988

https://www.flickr.com/photos/hotzeplotz/67495932/in/gallery-189870699@N02-72157715884590167

https://www.flickr.com/photos/repolco/46431567025/in/gallery-189870699@N02-72157715884590167

https://www.flickr.com/photos/levanrami/44709621625/in/gallery-189870699@N02-72157715884590167

https://www.flickr.com/photos/156515782@N02/49604265887/in/gallery-189870699@N02-72157715884590167

https://www.flickr.com/photos/christopherdombres/5397965371/in/gallery-189870699@N02-72157715884590167

https://www.flickr.com/photos/10413717@N08/4548816970/in/gallery-189870699@N02-72157715884590167

https://www.flickr.com/photos/charlottehenard/8296290551/in/gallery-189870699@N02-72157715884590167

https://www.flickr.com/photos/dave_fisher/4841419011/in/gallery-189870699@N02-72157715884590167

https://www.flickr.com/photos/97534175@N00/5489867060/in/gallery-189870699@N02-72157715884590167/

https://www.flickr.com/photos/97534175@N00/5489868202/in/gallery-189870699@N02-72157715884590167/

https://www.flickr.com/photos/88010770@N05/33731941188/in/gallery-189870699@N02-72157715884590167/

https://www.flickr.com/photos/156515782@N02/38969849552/in/gallery-189870699@N02-72157715884590167/

https://www.flickr.com/photos/anthonymason/17353582065/in/gallery-189870699@N02-72157715884590167

https://www.flickr.com/photos/fylin/387596912/in/gallery-189870699@N02-72157715884590167

https://www.flickr.com/photos/dedrawolff

Printed in Great Britain
by Amazon